The Scoop About Measuring Matter

by Tracy Nelson Maurer

Science Content Editor:
Shirley Duke

Educational Media

rourkeeducationalmedia.com

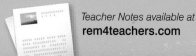

Teacher Notes available at
rem4teachers.com

Science Content Editor: Shirley Duke holds a bachelor's degree in biology and a master's degree in education from Austin College in Sherman, Texas. She taught science in Texas at all levels for twenty-five years before starting to write for children. Her science books include *You Can't Wear These Genes, Infections, Infestations, and Diseases, Enterprise STEM, Forces and Motion at Work, Environmental Disasters,* and *Gases.* She continues writing science books and also works as a science content editor.

www.rourkeeducationalmedia.com

Photo credits: Cover © Africa Studio, LVector; Pages 2/3 © Fedor Bobkov; Pages 4/5 © Hintau Aliaksei, alphaspirit; Pages 6/7 © Viktor88, somchaij, Kameel4u, agoxa, agrosse; Pages 8/9 © naluwan, KULISH VIKTORIIA, Lightspring, mack2happy; Pages 10/11 © Christy Thompson, Ari N, R. Gino Santa Maria; Pages 12/13 © Steve Cukrov, ggw1962, Stephen Mcsweeny; Pages 14/15 © Yuri Arcurs, LeCajun, JIANG HONGYAN; Pages 16/17 © Stanislav Komogorov, Evgeny Prokofyev, LianeM; Pages 18/19 © Fedor Bobkov, J.Schelkle; Pages 20/21 © Krzysztof Odziomek, Sergiy Zavgorodny, Geni, sgm

Editor: Kelli Hicks

My Science Library series produced by Blue Door Publishing, Florida for Rourke Educational Media.

Library of Congress PCN Data

Maurer, Tracy Nelson
 The Scoop about Measuring Matter / Tracy Nelson Maurer
     p. cm. -- (My Science Library)
 ISBN 978-1-61810-093-1 (Hard cover) (alk. paper)
 ISBN 978-1-61810-226-3 (Soft cover)
 Library of Congress Control Number: 2012930294

Rourke Educational Media
Printed in the United States of America,
North Mankato, Minnesota

rourkeeducationalmedia.com

customerservice@rourkeeducationalmedia.com • PO Box 643328 Vero Beach, Florida 32964

Table of Contents

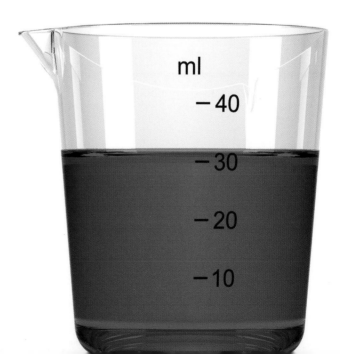

The Matter of It All

Everything in the universe is made up of matter, from things smaller than grains of sand to things larger than gigantic stars.

Matter is anything that has **mass**, meaning it is made of an amount of something and it takes up space.

Matter includes things you can't see, such as air. But, you can see that air takes up space if you blow up a balloon.

Matter of Fact:

Scientists may study the mass of matter in their work. For example, the mass of butterfly bodies could reveal clues about how they survive migration. By studying the survivors and those that died along the way, researchers might learn if body mass or food influenced those that live.

States that Matter

Tiny moving particles called molecules give matter its **physical properties**.

Matter of Fact:

Everything around us, both natural and manmade, is made up of atoms. An atom is the smallest particle of any substance. Millions of atoms exist in just one of your eyelashes. When two or more atoms bond, they form a molecule. This is a water molecule:

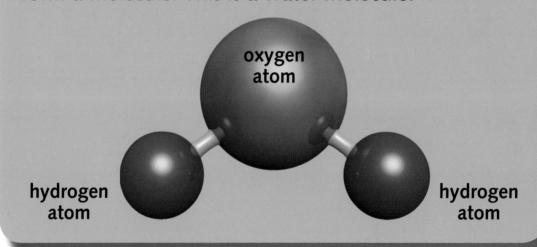

oxygen atom

hydrogen atom

hydrogen atom

Scientists know of five main physical properties, called **states**. Only three are common: solid, liquid, and gas. Super-cold Bose-Einstein condensates and plasmas are the two most recently discovered states.

solid

liquid

gas

Adding or removing pressure, motion, or heat changes matter from one state to another. But matter is matter in any state. Water is water if you add heat to make steam (gas) or remove heat to make ice (solid).

Plasmas help create the vibrant colors of the aurora borealis, or northern lights, and images on plasma TVs.

Aurora borealis over mountains in Tromso, Norway

Molecules in every state move all the time. Some move more slowly than others, such as molecules in a solid. Those molecules are tightly packed together, which gives the solid its definite shape. A solid doesn't need a container to hold its shape.

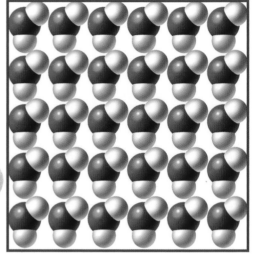

Stones are solids with very tightly packed molecules.

A liquid does not have a shape. It takes the shape of its container. Molecules in a liquid loosely flow under and over each other.

Liquid molecules slip around each other. This allows a liquid to flow from one shape to another.

Heat speeds up the motion of the gas molecules inside the balloon.

A gas, like a liquid, does not have a shape, but it completely fills the shape of its container. Fast-moving molecules in a gas have a lot of space between them and bounce off the container's walls.

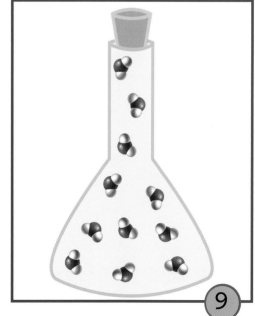

9

Measuring Units

Scientists measure matter using the International System of Units, based on the metric system. For example, the gram shows mass, or the amount of matter in an object. The liter shows the **volume**, or the amount of space the matter takes up.

Cooking with Volume

Like scientists, cooks use tools to measure volume. Most American cooks measure in ounces, cups, or quarts instead of metric units.

Approximate Liquid Measurements

American	Metric
1 tablespoon	15 mL
1/4 cup	59 mL
1/2 cup	118 mL
1 cup	237 mL
1 pint	473 mL
1 gallon	3.78 liters

Scientists measure mass using grams (g) and kilograms (kg). A gram is about the weight of a paper clip. A kilogram is about the weight of a baseball bat.

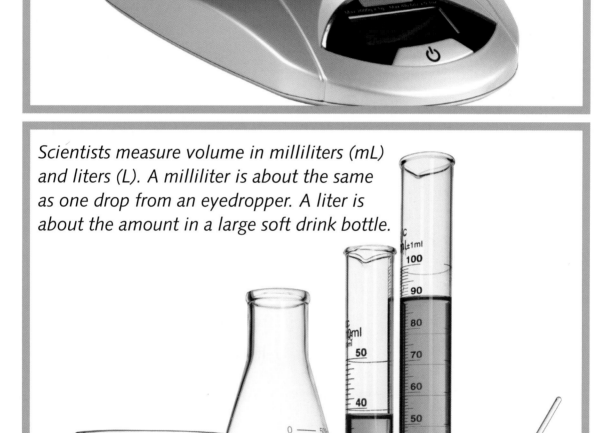

Scientists measure volume in milliliters (mL) and liters (L). A milliliter is about the same as one drop from an eyedropper. A liter is about the amount in a large soft drink bottle.

Common tools for measuring matter include a **graduated cylinder**, a flask, balance scale, ruler, and syringe or dropper.

Every tool must be carefully cleaned after each experiment. Matter left in a tool may change the results or create stinky or harmful mixtures. Scientists usually store tools in dust-free cabinets to keep them clean.

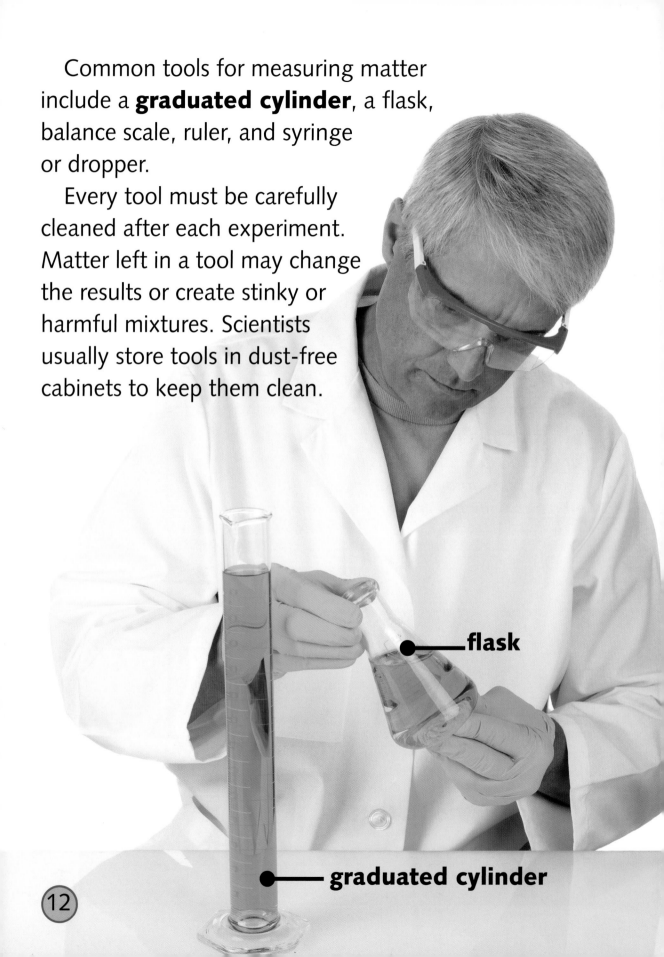

flask

graduated cylinder

In experiments, tools rarely cause mistakes. What does? The person measuring! Measure with care and always wear your safety gear.

Researchers often use special strengthened glass tools that won't melt in high heat or break at low temperatures.

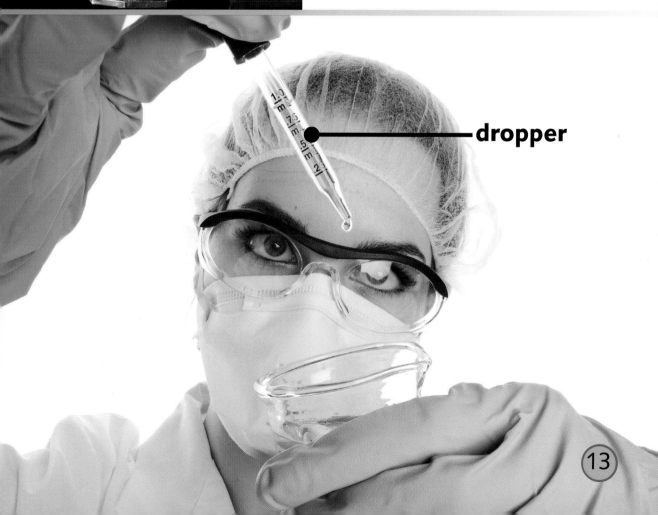

dropper

Measuring Mass

Mass and weight are different measurements. Your mass might be 30 kilograms (66 pounds) on Earth. Because space has no **gravity**, you would weigh 0 kilograms (0 pounds) there but your mass would still be 30 kilograms.

A body's mass on Earth stays the same in space.

mass = the amount of matter in an object

weight = gravity's pull on an object

A **spring scale** measures weight, or how much the spring moves down because of gravity's pull on the load.

A **balance scale** finds the mass of matter. A known mass is added to the pan on one side until that arm balances with the matter on the other arm. A triple-beam balance also measures mass, mostly in laboratories.

spring scale

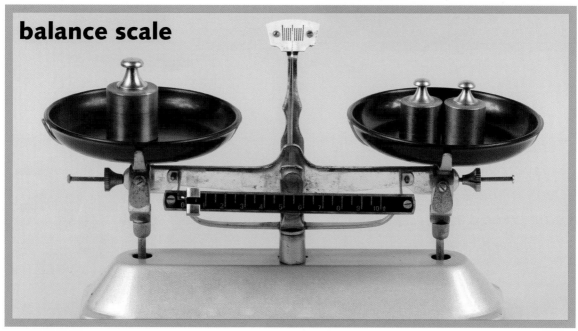

balance scale

The balance scale is the oldest known tool for finding mass or weight.

Mass stays the same when an object changes physical properties, such as state, color, or shape.

Mass also stays the same in a chemical reaction, when two combined materials change into an entirely new material.

The shape of the clay has changed. But the mass of the clay frog stays the same if you made it just using all of the green clay.

16

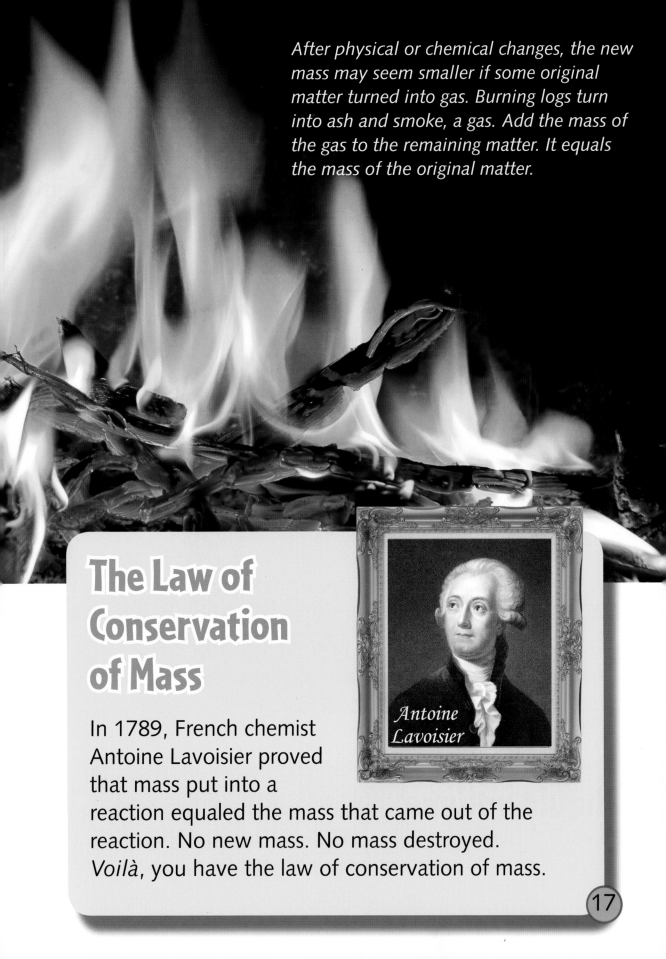

After physical or chemical changes, the new mass may seem smaller if some original matter turned into gas. Burning logs turn into ash and smoke, a gas. Add the mass of the gas to the remaining matter. It equals the mass of the original matter.

The Law of Conservation of Mass

In 1789, French chemist Antoine Lavoisier proved that mass put into a reaction equaled the mass that came out of the reaction. No new mass. No mass destroyed. *Voilà*, you have the law of conservation of mass.

Antoine Lavoisier

Measuring Volume

Matter takes up space. How much? Measure its volume.

When matter is a liquid, measure its volume with a measuring cup or graduated cylinder.

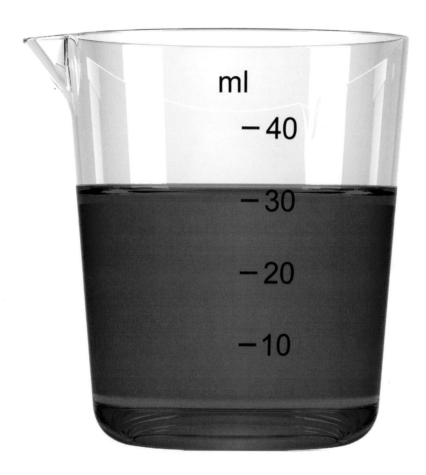

liquid volume = space filled in a graduated container in milliliters (mL)

When matter is a solid, measure its volume with a ruler and multiplication.

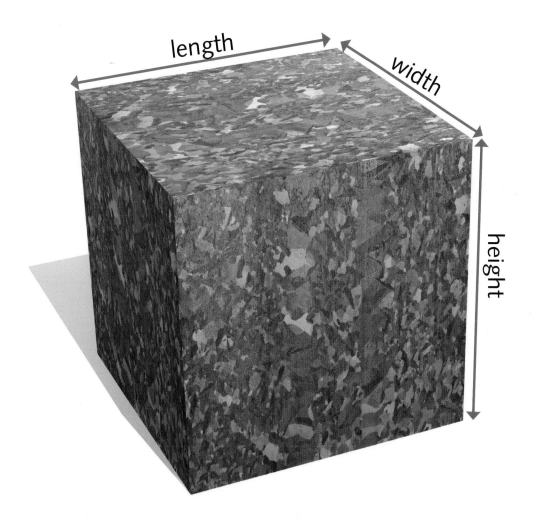

solid volume = length x width x height in centimeters (cm)

Measuring the mass of gas is tricky. Some gases can be measured by sucking them into a syringe. Scientists often use an electronic tool that controls the amount of gas flowing and that measures its volume.

A gas syringe in a laboratory is also called a glass collecting bottle. It can be used for measuring gas or liquid.

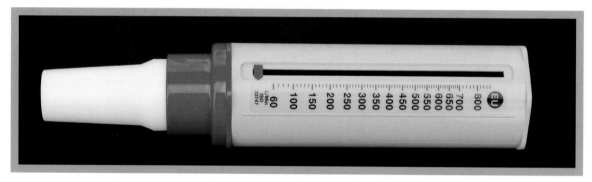

The force of the air rushing out of a person's lungs makes the red indicator move in this peak flow meter. It measures the amount of air moving out of the lungs. This measure shows if breathing is normal or if the airways are narrowing.

Matter of Fact:

People with asthma may use a peak flow meter to measure the rate or speed of gas flowing out from their lungs when they forcefully exhale. This allows doctors to track how well patients are breathing.

Gauges attached to scuba tanks measure the air inside. The gauges measure the volume of gas leaving the tank and show the volume of gas that is left in the tank.

Measuring matter helps scientists identify materials and understand more about the world. Careful measurements could mean better medicines, new products, or even a better cake at home!

Show What You Know

1. How do scientists measure matter?

2. Why do you think some cereal boxes and chip bags say, "sold by weight, not by volume"?

3. When might you measure volume at home?

Glossary

balance scale (BAL-uhnss SKALE): a tool used to measure how much something weighs

graduated cylinder (GRAJ-oo-ay-ted SIL-uhn-dur): a tall, round container with lines marked on it for measuring

gravity (GRAV-uh-tee): the pull on matter toward Earth's surface

mass (MASS): the measure of stuff, the something, of a substance

physical properties (FIZ-uh-kuhl PROP-ur-teez): qualities or traits something has

spring scale (SPRING SKALE): a type of scale that uses gravity and a spring to measure weight

states (STATES): the forms in which matter exists

volume (VOL-yuhm): the amount of space matter takes up

Index

Websites to Visit

www.chem4kids.com
www.sciencenewsforkids.org
http://www.tpt.org/newtons/index.php

About the Author

Tracy Nelson Maurer likes science
experiments, especially the cooking kind!
She lives in Minnesota with her husband
and two children. She holds an MFA in
Writing for Children and Young Adults
from Hamline University.

Ask The Author!
www.rem4students.com